Ms Pineda

Word Wall Practice!
High Frequency Words!
Level 1 (128 words)

This workbook contains skill-based worksheets and reproducible word cards for the first 128 High Frequency Words:

a ⑪	call ⑤	give	it	old	than	way	zero
about	can	go ⑤	like	on ⑧	that	we	one
after	car	good	long ②	or	the	went	two
all	come	had	look ②	other	their	were	three
am	could	has	made	out	them	what	four
an	day	have	make	over	then	when	five
and	did ④	he ⑨	many	part	there	where	six
are	do	her	may ⑦	play	these	which	seven
as	down	here	me	ride	they	who	eight
ask	each	him	more	run	this	why	nine
at	eat ②	his	my	said	time	will	ten
be ⑥	find	how	new	saw	to	with	
been	for ④	I	no ④	see	up	word	
big	from	if	not	she	us	would	
boy	fun	in ⑥	now	so	use	you	
but	get	into	of	some	want	your	
by	girl	is	off	tell	was		

Written by
Richard W. Sevaly, M.S. Ed.

Illustrated by
Karen Sevaly

Copyright © 1999
Teacher's Friend Publications, Inc.
All rights reserved.
Printed in the United States of America
Published by Teacher's Friend Publications, Inc.
3240 Trade Center Dr., Riverside, CA 92507

ISBN-0-57882-023-5

teacher's friend publications

Reproduction of these materials for commercial resale or distribution to an entire school or school district is strictly prohibited. Pages may be duplicated for one individual classroom set only. Material may not be reproduced for other purposes without the prior written permission of the publisher.

Table of Contents

	Page
A Word About This Practice Book!	3
"I Can Read These Words!" Chart	5
Word Wall Activities	6
Word Wall Whiz Kid Award and Incentive Notes	7
Practice Sheet	8
Lesson 1 - (a, and, of, the, to)	9
Lesson 2 - (in, is, it, that, you)	12
Lesson 3 - (are, for, he, on, was)	15
Lesson 4 - (as, his, I, they, with)	18
Lesson 5 - (at, be, from, have, this)	21
Lesson 6 - (by, had, one, or, word)	24
Lesson 7 - (all, but, not, were, what)	27
Lesson 8 - (can, said, we, when, your)	30
Lesson 9 - (an, each, there, use, which)	33
Lesson 10 - (do, how, if, she, their)	36
Lesson 11 - (about, other, out, up, will)	39
Lesson 12 - (many, so, them, then, these)	42
Lesson 13 - (her, like, make, some, would)	45
Lesson 14 - (has, him, into, look, time)	48
Lesson 15 - (ask, go, more, see, two)	51
Lesson 16 - (big, boy, could, no, way)	54
Lesson 17 - (been, eat, girl, my, than)	57
Lesson 18 - (call, car, find, now, who)	60
Lesson 19 - (day, did, down, get, long)	63
Lesson 20 - (come, good, made, may, part)	66
Lesson 21 - (fun, here, new, off, old)	69
Lesson 22 - (run, tell, us, went, why)	72
Lesson 23 - (give, me, over, saw, want)	75
Lesson 24 - (after, am, play, ride, where)	78
Lesson 25 - (zero, one, two, three, four, five)	81
Lesson 26 - (six, seven, eight, nine, ten)	84
Answer Keys	87
Create-Your-Own-Worksheets!	93

Word Wall Practice High Frequency Words!

Teaching With Word Walls!

The pages in this workbook have been designed to be used independently or as a supplement to the lessons taught using a classroom Word Wall. The words used in this practice book coordinate with the word cards contained in the Teacher's Friend Word Wall Word Set - High Frequency Words - Level 1.

Please note: One way to help students identify confusing words is with a visual cue. With this in mind, we have framed the words in each lesson by emphasizing the ascending and descending letters. In this way a student will quickly recognize the difference between similar words and be better able to remember each word's correct spelling.

Whether you use a Word Wall or not, you will find that these worksheets and student word cards will help students recognize and practice essential sight words necessary to their reading and spelling progress.

Teaching High Frequency Words!

Learning to read, write and spell high frequency words is probably the most important skill needed by young learners. It is essential that beginning readers master these words as "sight" words in order to progress in their education. Even though some high frequency words can be sounded out phonetically, children need to immediately recognize them by sight without any hesitation. In this regard, all high frequency words in Teacher's Friend Word Wall Word Sets and Practice Books are taught as "sight" words.

Most reading experts agree that over 50% of all written material consists of the top 100 (or so) high frequency words! It is recommended that first graders master the top 100 high frequency words, second graders the top 200 and third graders the top 300. When students master each of the top 300 high frequency words, they will be able to read, write and spell over 65% of all written material! In other words, they will be able to successfully read and write more that half of anything they want! That includes text books, newspapers, story books and so on.

The high frequency words worksheets contained in this book do not supplant the adopted reading and phonics program you are teaching in your classroom. We do recommend that you post the high frequency words on a Word Wall giving students consistent, visual reinforcement of the words they most need for reading, writing and spelling as a supplement to your reading program.

Which Words Do You Teach First?

It is important to introduce high frequency words in the order they will most frequently appear in classroom reading materials. We have organized each group of five words in the order studies have indicated as the most often used words in reading and writing. It is our suggestion that you introduce them in the order as they appear in this Word Wall Practice Book. (To maintain a high success rate, we recommend that only 5-10 words be taught per week.)

The Student Word Cards!

In this book you will find a set of reproducible, interactive word cards for each group of five high frequency words. Duplicate the word card page onto colored index paper and give one page to each student. Instruct the students to trace each word and trace the frame around it. Students can then cut the word cards apart and use them as flash cards with a friend or take them home to practice with a parent.

The Worksheets!

The worksheets in this book (High Frequency Words) are designed for the beginning learner. You will find that most students can do the worksheets with very little coaching from the teacher after the introductory lesson. Please notice that each page asks the student to "read, whisper and finger-clap each word in the word box before beginning." This multi-sensory word practice will "quietly" help reinforce the teaching you have done using the Word Wall. It also offers an effective way for you to visually monitor your students as to whether they are on task.

With or without the use of a Word Wall, these worksheets provide an excellent tool to review and practice words previously taught. They can effectively be used by both teacher and parent.

Note: The practice worksheets are designed for students to use block or manuscript lettering.

Steps to Word Wall Practice!

Teach and reinforce the words on your Word Wall by using these visual, auditory and kinesthetic steps.

1. Instruct all students to look at the first word on the wall.
2. Read and spell the word aloud.
3. Have students read and spell the word in unison.
4. Write the word on the class board emphasizing correct form. Read and spell the word as you write it.
5. Instruct students to write the word, using correct form, on their Word Wall Practice Sheet.
6. Repeat all five steps for each word.
7. Following your lead, ask students to check each word for spelling and proper form by drawing around the shape of each word.

Each day, repeat all steps using the same words. At the end of the each week, practice and review previously studied words from the Word Wall lessons. The next week, begin a new lesson with new words and follow the same procedures.

Here is a simple lesson plan for using both your classroom Word Wall and the Word Wall Practice Worksheets and Word Cards contained in this book.

Monday	Word Wall Practice	Specific Introduction of New Words
Tuesday	Word Wall Practice	Student Word Cards from the Word Wall Practice Book
Wednesday	Word Wall Practice	Practice Worksheet, first page
Thursday	Word Wall Practice	Practice Worksheet, second page
Friday	Word Wall Review	Give your own spelling test (include review words)

Spell Check!

On the bottom of the first page of each lesson, you will notice a directive labeled Spell which directs students to "turn the page over and write the words from the word box from memory." This will help students acquire visualization skills needed to recognize words and improve spelling. Please remind students that if they become stumped on a word, they can always refer to the classroom Word Wall. Instruct students to immediately check their spelling of the words. If they find a misspelled word, direct them to write that word correctly three additional times. This is especially important so students do not continue to practice a misspelled word.

Teacher's Friend Publications, Inc. ©

Name _____

"I can read these words!"

High Frequency Words - Level 1

☐ a	☐ day	☐ his	☐ of	☐ their	☐ which
☐ about	☐ did	☐ how	☐ off	☐ them	☐ who
☐ after	☐ do	☐ I	☐ old	☐ then	☐ why
☐ all	☐ down	☐ if	☐ on	☐ there	☐ will
☐ am	☐ each	☐ in	☐ or	☐ these	☐ with
☐ an	☐ eat	☐ into	☐ other	☐ they	☐ word
☐ and	☐ find	☐ is	☐ out	☐ this	☐ would
☐ are	☐ for	☐ it	☐ over	☐ time	☐ you
☐ as	☐ from	☐ like	☐ part	☐ to	☐ your
☐ ask	☐ fun	☐ long	☐ play	☐ two	
☐ at	☐ get	☐ look	☐ ride	☐ up	☐ zero
☐ be	☐ girl	☐ made	☐ run	☐ us	☐ one
☐ been	☐ give	☐ make	☐ said	☐ use	☐ two
☐ big	☐ go	☐ many	☐ saw	☐ want	☐ three
☐ boy	☐ good	☐ may	☐ see	☐ was	☐ four
☐ but	☐ had	☐ me	☐ she	☐ way	☐ five
☐ by	☐ has	☐ more	☐ so	☐ we	☐ six
☐ call	☐ have	☐ my	☐ some	☐ went	☐ seven
☐ can	☐ he	☐ new	☐ tell	☐ were	☐ eight
☐ car	☐ her	☐ no	☐ than	☐ what	☐ nine
☐ come	☐ here	☐ not	☐ that	☐ when	☐ ten
☐ could	☐ him	☐ now	☐ the	☐ where	

Word Wall Activities! High Frequency Words!

Activities for This Week's Words!

- Find this week's words in your reading book, library book or magazine.
- Write each word in good form. Draw a frame around each word's shape with a different color.
- Write a complete sentence using each word.
- Write the words for this week in alphabetical order.
- Make flashcards using the words and ask a friend to quiz you.

Activities for Word Wall Words!
Using all the words on the Word Wall:

- Find all the words with the same number of syllables, and write them on your paper.
- List all the words with the same beginning letter.
- List all the words with the same ending letter.
- List all the words with the same short vowel sound.
- List all the words with the same long vowel sound.
- Choose one word with at least five letters. Use the same letters to make other words, and write as many as you can.
- Write a paragraph using five words from the Word Wall.
- List all the words with the same number of letters.
- Select ten words, and write them in good form on your paper. Draw a frame around each word's shape.
- Write one sentence using three words from the wall, and draw a picture to illustrate it.

_____

**has mastered
High Frequency Words - Level 1!**

_____ _____

Name _____

can read these words!

_____
_____
_____
_____
_____

Name _____

needs help learning these words!

_____
_____
_____
_____
_____

My Word Wall Practice Sheet!

Name _____

1.

2.

3.

4.

5.

"I can write the Word Wall Words!"

Give your students extra practice by reproducing this page on the back of the worksheets contained in this book.

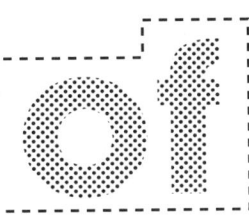 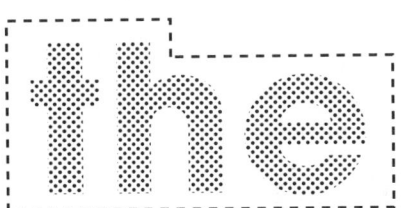

High Frequency Word Cards

For each word:
- ☐ Trace the word.
- ☐ Trace the frame.

Cut the word cards apart and practice reading the words with a friend.

Teacher's Friend Publications, Inc. ©   TF2425 Word Wall Practice! High Frequency Words Level 1

Name _____

Word Box
| a | and | of |
| the | to | |

Read, whisper and finger-clap the words in the word box before you begin.

Write the words from the word box and draw a frame around each word.

1. _____
2. _____
3. _____
4. _____
5. _____

Can you read and spell these words?

7. Circle the words from the word box and place an "X" on each word that does *not* appear in the word box.

of	big
to	go
at	the
and	be
bad	a

6. Unscramble this word from the word box.

n d a

_____

SPELL ✓

Now, turn this page over and write the words from the word box from memory. Did you spell each word correctly?

Name _____

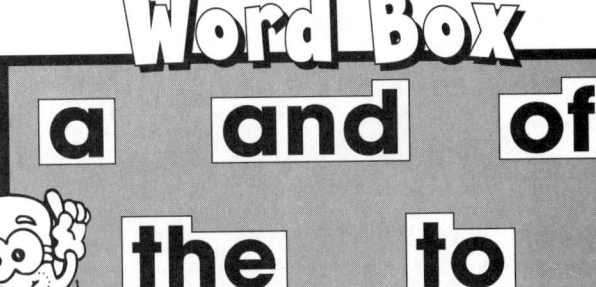

Read, whisper and finger-clap the words in the word box before you begin.

Trace the gray letters and add the missing letters to make each word from the word box. Trace the frame around each word.

Can you read and spell these words?

1. _ n _
2. _ o _
3. _ _
4. _ _ e
5. _ o _

Bonus Activity!

Circle the word in the sentence below that also appears in the word box.

Dan went to play.

6. Circle the words below that appear in the word box. Place an "X" on each word that does not appear in the word box. (Words may appear more than once.)

the	stop	and	a
of	a	the	go
a	to	and	he
to	of	me	and

Teacher's Friend Publications, Inc. ©

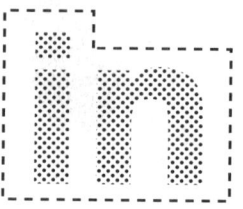 

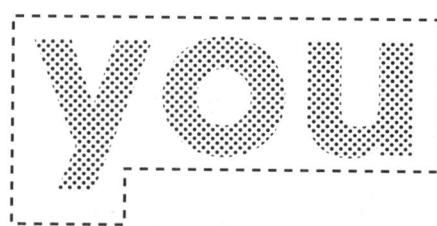

High Frequency Word Cards

For each word:
- ☐ Trace the word.
- ☐ Trace the frame.

Cut the word cards apart and practice reading the words with a friend.

Name _____

Word Box

in	is	it
that	you	

Read, whisper and finger-clap the words in the word box before you begin.

Write the words from the word box and draw a frame around each word.

1. _____
2. _____
3. _____
4. _____
5. _____

Can you read and spell these words?

6. Unscramble this word from the word box.

u o y

_____

SPELL ✓

Now, turn this page over and write the words from the word box from memory. Did you spell each word correctly?

7. Find 5 words from the word box in the puzzle. Circle the words.

i	t	p	t	x	b	h	g	i
v	q	c	c	r	i	s	j	y
a	i	n	r	s	b	b	s	o
a	b	b	c	t	h	a	t	u

Teacher's Friend Publications, Inc. © 13 TF2425 Word Wall Practice! High Frequency Words Level 1

Name _____

Read, whisper and finger-clap the words in the word box before you begin.

Word Box
| in | is | it |
| that | you | |

Can you read and spell these words?

1. Trace the grey words and frames around each word from the word box. Draw a frame around each matching word.

is	is	on	if
it	at	to	it
that	the	they	that
in	in	on	am
you	yes	you	your

2. Find the words from the word box. Frame the word. Write the word in the open frame and trace the frame.

it	to	at	
no	in	on	
yet	you	yes	
on	if	is	
that	they	the	

Teacher's Friend Publications, Inc. ©   14   TF2425 Word Wall Practice! High Frequency Words Level 1

 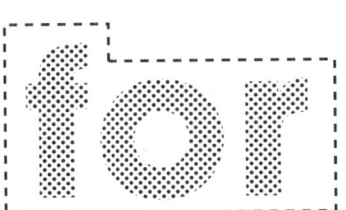

High Frequency Word Cards

For each word:
- ☐ Trace the word.
- ☐ Trace the frame.

Cut the word cards apart and practice reading the words with a friend.

Name _____

Read, whisper and finger-clap the words in the word box before you begin.

Word Box
are for he
on   was

Write the words from the word box and draw a frame around each word.

1. _____
2. _____
3. _____
4. _____
5. _____

Can you read and spell these words?

7. Circle the words from the word box and place an "X" on each word that does *not* appear in the word box.

on   an
are   and
we   was
he   the
of   for

6. Unscramble this word from the word box.

a s w

_____

SPELL ✓

Now, turn this page over and write the words from the word box from memory. Did you spell each word correctly?

Teacher's Friend Publications, Inc. ©   16   TF2425 Word Wall Practice! High Frequency Words Level 1

Name _____

Word Box
are for he
on was

Read, whisper and finger-clap the words in the word box before you begin.

Read each sentence.
Find a word from the word box in each sentence and circle it.

Can you read and spell these words?

1. We are going to lunch.

2. Jan was in line.

3. Come and play on the swing.

4. Can he play with us?

5. Go for the fun of it.

6. Unscramble these words from the word box.

f r o _____

e h _____

e a r _____

Teacher's Friend Publications, Inc. ©   17   TF2425 Word Wall Practice! High Frequency Words Level 1

 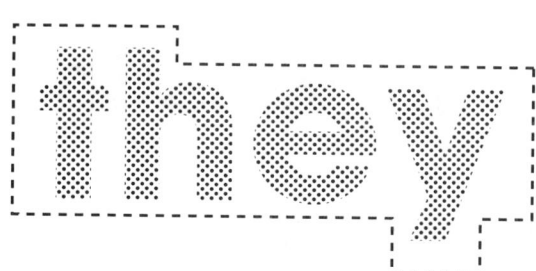

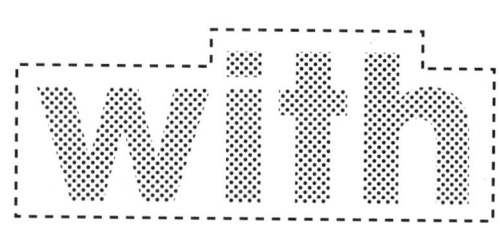 

High Frequency Word Cards

For each word:
- ☐ Trace the word.
- ☐ Trace the frame.

Cut the word cards apart and practice reading the words with a friend.

Name _____

Word Box

| as | his | I |
| they | with | |

Read, whisper and finger-clap the words in the word box before you begin.

Write the words from the word box and draw a frame around each word.

1. _____
2. _____
3. _____
4. _____
5. _____

Can you read and spell these words?

6. **Unscramble this word from the word box.**

t h i w

_____

SPELL ✓

Now, turn this page over and write the words from the word box from memory. Did you spell each word correctly?

7. **Find 5 words from the word box in the puzzle. Circle the words.**

I	d	p	t	x	a	h	g	t
v	q	c	h	i	s	b	j	h
a	e	g	r	c	b	b	s	e
w	i	t	h	j	u	e	x	y

Teacher's Friend Publications, Inc. ©

Name _____

Read, whisper and finger-clap the words in the word box before you begin.

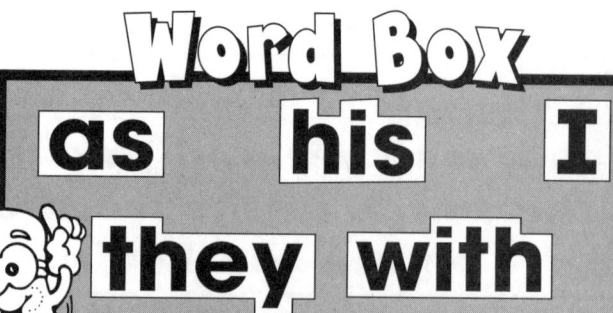

Word Box
as   his   I
they   with

Trace the gray letters and add the missing letters to make each word from the word box. Trace the frame around each word.

Can you read and spell these words?

1. _ I _
2. _ _
3. _ s _
4. _ _ t _ _
5. h _ _

Bonus Activity!

Circle the word in the sentence below that also appears in the word box.

Can we go with you?

6. Circle the words below that appear in the word box. Place an "X" on each word that does not appear in the word box. (Words may appear more than once.)

I	the	with	as
they	his	I	and
of	as	his	they
with	they	that	his

Teacher's Friend Publications, Inc. ©

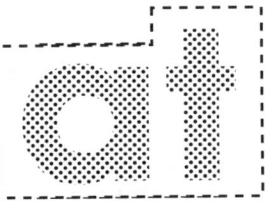
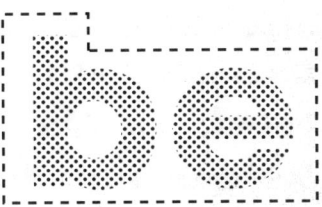

High Frequency Word Cards

For each word:
- ☐ Trace the word.
- ☐ Trace the frame.

Cut the word cards apart and practice reading the words with a friend.

Name _____

Read, whisper and finger-clap the words in the word box before you begin.

Word Box
at be from
have this

Write the words from the word box and draw a frame around each word.

1. _____
2. _____
3. _____
4. _____
5. _____

Can you read and spell these words?

7. Circle the words from the word box and place an "X" on each word that does *not* appear in the word box.

be   and
the   this
that   from
have   he
at   of

6. Unscramble this word from the word box.

a v h e

_____

Now, turn this page over and write the words from the word box from memory. Did you spell each word correctly?

Name _____

Read, whisper and finger-clap the words in the word box before you begin.

Word Box

at   be   from
have   this

Can you read and spell these words?

1. Trace the grey words and frames around each word from the word box. Draw a frame around each matching word.

be	been	by
hot	hold	have
this	that	they
of	from	for
and	at	are

2. Find the words from the word box. Frame the word. Write the word in the open frame and trace the frame.

from	fat	of
big	be	bat
have	his	hot
they	the	this
to	it	at

Teacher's Friend Publications, Inc. ©   23   TF2425 Word Wall Practice! High Frequency Words Level 1

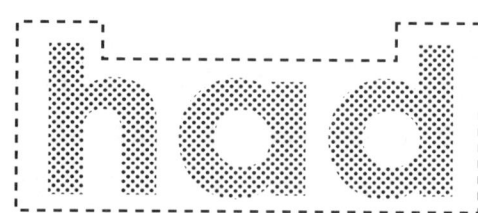

High Frequency Word Cards

For each word:
- ☐ Trace the word.
- ☐ Trace the frame.

Cut the word cards apart and practice reading the words with a friend.

Name _____

Word Box
by had one or word

Read, whisper and finger-clap the words in the word box before you begin.

Write the words from the word box and draw a frame around each word.

1. _____
2. _____
3. _____
4. _____
5. _____

Can you read and spell these words?

6. Unscramble this word from the word box.

d r w o

_____

SPELL

Now, turn this page over and write the words from the word box from memory. Did you spell each word correctly?

7. Find 5 words from the word box in the puzzle. Circle the words.

o	r	p	t	w	h	a	d	i
v	b	c	c	o	a	b	j	w
a	y	g	r	r	b	b	s	k
a	b	b	c	d	u	o	n	e

Teacher's Friend Publications, Inc. ©   25   TF2425 Word Wall Practice! High Frequency Words Level 1

Name _____

Read, whisper and finger-clap the words in the word box before you begin.

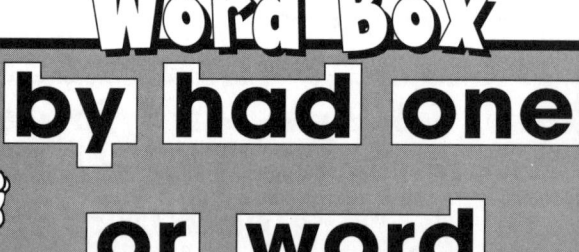

Word Box
by had one or word

Can you read and spell these words?

Read each sentence. Find a word from the word box in each sentence and circle it.

1. Come by and see me.
2. Read this word for me.
3. Do you like red or green?
4. I had to eat my lunch.
5. May I have a blue one?

6. Unscramble these words from the word box.

d h a _____

n o e _____

y b _____

Teacher's Friend Publications, Inc. ©   TF2425 Word Wall Practice! High Frequency Words Level 1

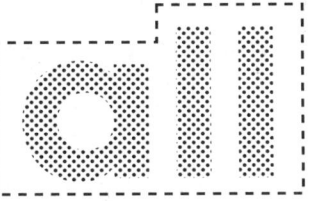 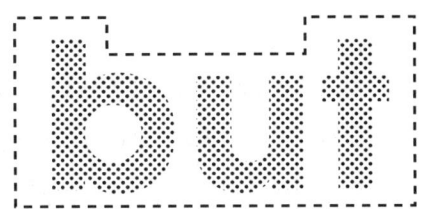

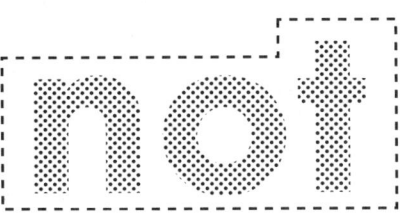 

High Frequency Word Cards

For each word:
- ☐ Trace the word.
- ☐ Trace the frame.

Cut the word cards apart and practice reading the words with a friend.

Name _____

Read, whisper and finger-clap the words in the word box before you begin.

Word Box
all but not were what

Write the words from the word box and draw a frame around each word.

1. _____
2. _____
3. _____
4. _____
5. _____

Can you read and spell these words?

7. Circle the words from the word box and place an "X" on each word that does *not* appear in the word box.

were   word
but   by
on   not
all   at
with   what

6. Unscramble this word from the word box.

a t w h

_____
_____

Now, turn this page over and write the words from the word box from memory. Did you spell each word correctly?

Name _____

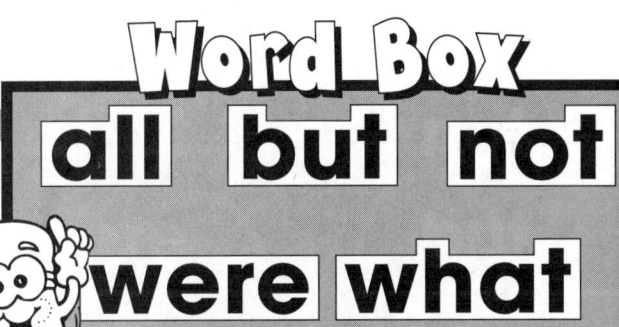

Word Box
all but not
were what

Read, whisper and finger-clap the words in the word box before you begin.

Trace the gray letters and add the missing letters to make each word from the word box. Trace the frame around each word.

Can you read and spell these words?

1. _ l _
2. _ w _ _ _
3. _ _ o _
4. w _ _ _
5. _ u _

Bonus Activity!

Circle the word in the sentence below that also appears in the word box.

We were about to go.

6. Circle the words below that appear in the word box. Place an "X" on each word that does not appear in the word box. (Words may appear more than once.)

not	but	have	all
what	were	all	had
from	all	what	not
were	this	were	but

Teacher's Friend Publications, Inc. ©   29   TF2425 Word Wall Practice! High Frequency Words Level 1

can | said

we | when

your

High Frequency Word Cards

For each word:
- ☐ Trace the word.
- ☐ Trace the frame.

Cut the word cards apart and practice reading the words with a friend.

Name _____

Word Box
can said we when your

Read, whisper and finger-clap the words in the word box before you begin.

Write the words from the word box and draw a frame around each word.

1. _____
2. _____
3. _____
4. _____
5. _____

Can you read and spell these words?

6. Unscramble this word from the word box.

d s i a

_____

SPELL ✓
Now, turn this page over and write the words from the word box from memory. Did you spell each word correctly?

7. Find 5 words from the word box in the puzzle. Circle the words.

```
s c a n y b h w e
a q c c o a b j w
i e g l u b b s k
d b b c r w h e n
```

Teacher's Friend Publications, Inc. ©   31   TF2425 Word Wall Practice! High Frequency Words Level 1

Name _____

Read, whisper and finger-clap the words in the word box before you begin.

Word Box
can said we
when your

Can you read and spell these words?

1. Trace the grey words and frames around each word from the word box. Draw a frame around each matching word.

we	we	was	with
your	yes	you	your
said	save	said	safe
can	can	came	come
when	what	when	was

2. Find the words from the word box. Frame the word. Write the word in the open frame and trace the frame.

saw	say	said
when	was	word
way	what	we
yard	your	you
can	and	are

Teacher's Friend Publications, Inc. ©   TF2425 Word Wall Practice! High Frequency Words Level 1

an

each

there

use

which

High Frequency Word Cards

For each word:
- ☐ Trace the word.
- ☐ Trace the frame.

Cut the word cards apart and practice reading the words with a friend.

Name _____

Word Box
an each use
there which

Read, whisper and finger-clap the words in the word box before you begin.

Write the words from the word box and draw a frame around each word.

1. _____
2. _____
3. _____
4. _____
5. _____

Can you read and spell these words?

7. Circle the words from the word box and place an "X" on each word that does *not* appear in the word box.

an   and
use   us
when   which
there that
eat   each

6. Unscramble this word from the word box.

c h w h i

_____

Now, turn this page over and write the words from the word box from memory. Did you spell each word correctly?

Teacher's Friend Publications, Inc. ©   34   TF2425 Word Wall Practice! High Frequency Words Level 1

Name _____

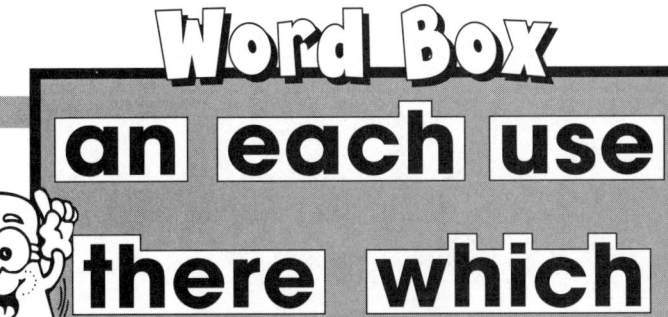

Word Box
an each use
there which

Read, whisper and finger-clap the words in the word box before you begin.

Read each sentence.
Find a word from the word box in each sentence and circle it.

Can you read and spell these words?

1. You may have one of each kind.

2. Are there any pencils in the cup?

3. You can use a red marker.

4. I don't know which one is best.

5. I ate an apple for lunch.

6. Unscramble these words from the word box.

eerth _____

e s u _____

chea _____

Teacher's Friend Publications, Inc. ©   35   TF2425 Word Wall Practice! High Frequency Words Level 1

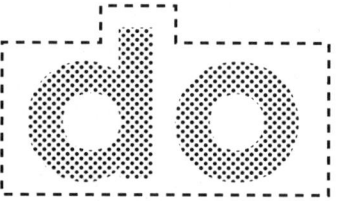 

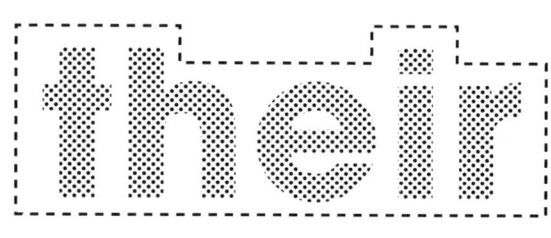 

High Frequency Word Cards

For each word:
- ☐ Trace the word.
- ☐ Trace the frame.

Cut the word cards apart and practice reading the words with a friend.

Teacher's Friend Publications, Inc. ©   36   TF2425 Word Wall Practice! High Frequency Words Level 1

Name _____

Word Box

do   how   if
she   their

Read, whisper and finger-clap the words in the word box before you begin.

Write the words from the word box and draw a frame around each word.

1. _____
2. _____
3. _____
4. _____
5. _____

Can you read and spell these words?

6. Unscramble this word from the word box.

e i r h t

_____

Now, turn this page over and write the words from the word box from memory. Did you spell each word correctly?

7. Find 5 words from the word box in the puzzle. Circle the words.

i	d	s	t	x	b	h	g	i
f	q	h	c	t	h	e	i	r
a	e	e	r	a	o	b	s	d
a	b	b	c	j	w	e	x	o

Teacher's Friend Publications, Inc. ©   37   TF2425 Word Wall Practice! High Frequency Words Level 1

Name _____

Read, whisper and finger-clap the words in the word box before you begin.

Word Box
**do how if
she their**

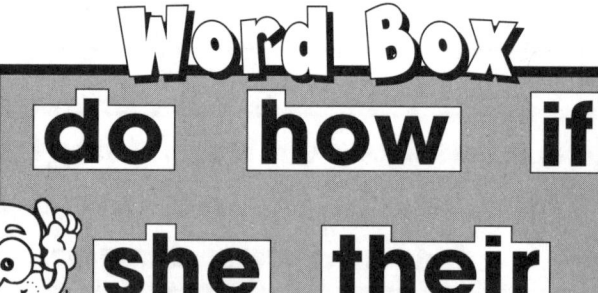

Trace the gray letters and add the missing letters to make each word from the word box. Trace the frame around each word.

Can you read and spell these words?

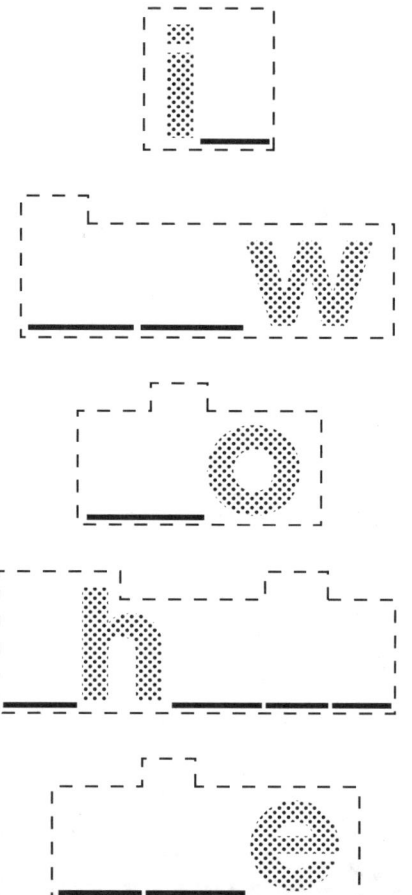

1. i_
2. __w
3. __o_
4. __h___
5. ___e

Bonus Activity!

Circle the word in the sentence below that also appears in the word box.

Take their cat back home.

6. Circle the words below that appear in the word box. Place an "X" on each word that does not appear in the word box. (Words may appear more than once.)

if	she	their	each
their	there	if	she
how	do	their	use
from	how	she	do

Teacher's Friend Publications, Inc. © 38 TF2425 Word Wall Practice! High Frequency Words Level 1

 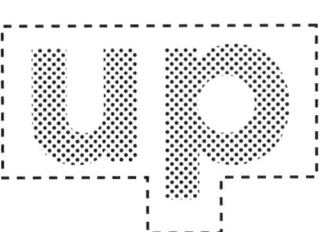

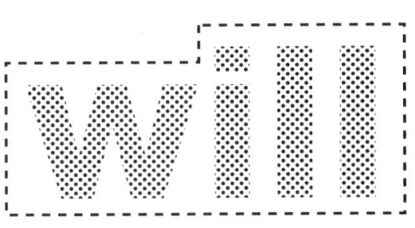 

High Frequency Word Cards

For each word:
- ☐ Trace the word.
- ☐ Trace the frame.

Cut the word cards apart and practice reading the words with a friend.

Name _____

Word Box
about other out up will

Read, whisper and finger-clap the words in the word box before you begin.

Write the words from the word box and draw a frame around each word.

1. _____
2. _____
3. _____
4. _____
5. _____

Can you read and spell these words?

6. Unscramble this word from the word box.

t a o u b

7. Circle the words from the word box and place an "X" on each word that does *not* appear in the word box.

up   use

were   will

one   other

about   out

have   from

SPELL ✓

Now, turn this page over and write the words from the word box from memory. Did you spell each word correctly?

Name _____

Read, whisper and finger-clap the words in the word box before you begin.

Word Box
**about other
out up will**

Can you read and spell these words?

1. Trace the grey words and frames around each word from the word box. Draw a frame around each matching word.

up	use	put
their	that	other
how	out	had
will	with	were
have	about	and

(trace: up, other, out, will, about)

2. Find the words from the word box. Frame the word. Write the word in the open frame and trace the frame.

out	how	but
with	what	will
their	other	there
that	from	about
up	it	at

Teacher's Friend Publications, Inc. ©

many | so

them | then

these

High Frequency Word Cards

For each word:
- ☐ Trace the word.
- ☐ Trace the frame.

Cut the word cards apart and practice reading the words with a friend.

Name _____

Word Box
many so them
then these

Read, whisper and finger-clap the words in the word box before you begin.

Write the words from the word box and draw a frame around each word.

1. _____
2. _____
3. _____
4. _____
5. _____

Can you read and spell these words?

6. Unscramble this word from the word box.

a n y m

_____

SPELL ✓
Now, turn this page over and write the words from the word box from memory. Did you spell each word correctly?

7. Find 5 words from the word box in the puzzle. Circle the words.

s o p t x b h g t
v q c c t h e m h
a e m a n y b s e
t h e s e u e x n

Teacher's Friend Publications, Inc. ©   43   TF2425 Word Wall Practice! High Frequency Words Level 1

Name _____

Read, whisper and finger-clap the words in the word box before you begin.

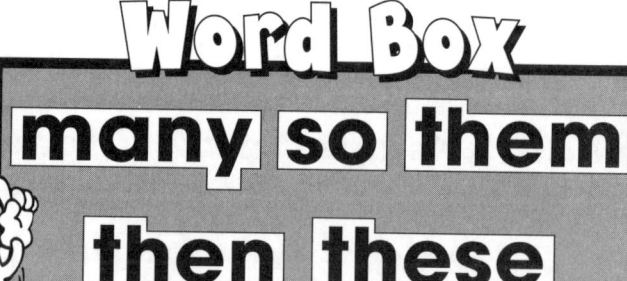

Word Box
many so them
then these

Read each sentence.
Find a word from the word box in each sentence and circle it.

Can you read and spell these words?

1. Do not take that many.

2. He will go with them.

3. I will go to bed and then sleep.

4. I am so happy!

5. Are these your new shoes?

6. Unscramble these words from the word box.

ethn _____

mhte _____

eesth _____

Teacher's Friend Publications, Inc. ©   44   TF2425 Word Wall Practice! High Frequency Words Level 1

her

like

make

some

would

High Frequency Word Cards

For each word:
- ☐ Trace the word.
- ☐ Trace the frame.

Cut the word cards apart and practice reading the words with a friend.

Name _____

Read, whisper and finger-clap the words in the word box before you begin.

Word Box
her like make
some would

Can you read and spell these words?

Write the words from the word box and draw a frame around each word.

1. _____
2. _____
3. _____
4. _____
5. _____

6. Unscramble this word from the word box.

l d o w u

_____

7. Circle the words from the word box and place an "X" on each word that does *not* appear in the word box.

some   said

make   many

her   how

live   like

word   would

Now, turn this page over and write the words from the word box from memory. Did you spell each word correctly?

Name _____

Read, whisper and finger-clap the words in the word box before you begin.

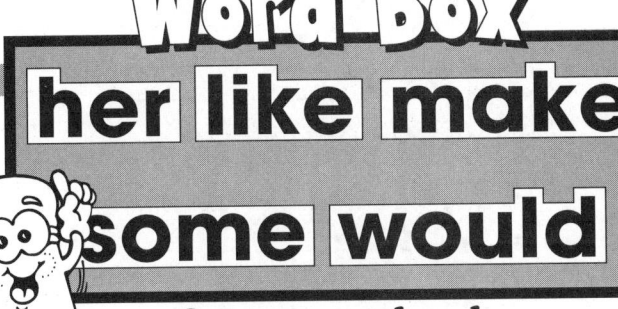

Word Box
her like make
some would

Trace the gray letters and add the missing letters to make each word from the word box. Trace the frame around each word.

Can you read and spell these words?

1. __ o __ __

2. __ k __

3. __ __ r

4. __ __ l __

5. __ __ __ e

Bonus Activity!

Circle the words in the sentence below that also appear in the word box.

I would like to play ball.

6. Circle the words below that appear in the word box. Place an "X" on each word that does not appear in the word box. (Words may appear more than once.)

like	some	then	make
make	her	these	would
their	would	some	like
some	like	her	your

Teacher's Friend Publications, Inc. ©   47   TF2425 Word Wall Practice! High Frequency Words Level 1

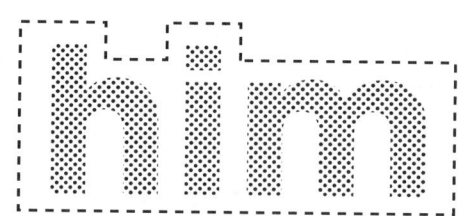
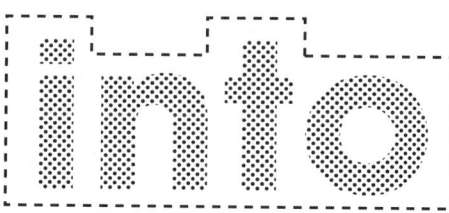
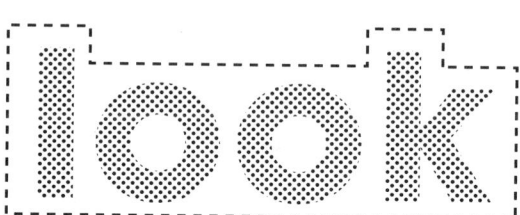
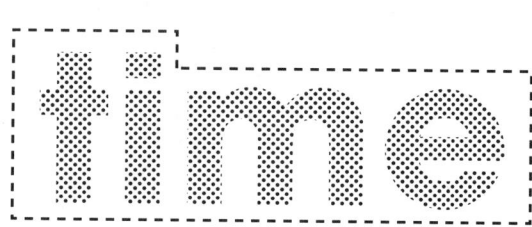

High Frequency Word Cards

For each word:
- ☐ Trace the word.
- ☐ Trace the frame.

Cut the word cards apart and practice reading the words with a friend.

Teacher's Friend Publications, Inc. ©   48   TF2425 Word Wall Practice! High Frequency Words Level 1

Name _____

Word Box
has | him | into
look | time

Read, whisper and finger-clap the words in the word box before you begin.

Write the words from the word box and draw a frame around each word.

1. _____
2. _____
3. _____
4. _____
5. _____

Can you read and spell these words?

6. **Unscramble this word from the word box.**

m e i t

_____

SPELL ✓

Now, turn this page over and write the words from the word box from memory. Did you spell each word correctly?

7. **Find 5 words from the word box in the puzzle. Circle the words.**

i n t o x b h g i
h q c c r l o o k
a e h i m b b s k
s t i m e u e x h

Teacher's Friend Publications, Inc. ©   49   TF2425 Word Wall Practice! High Frequency Words Level 1

Name _____

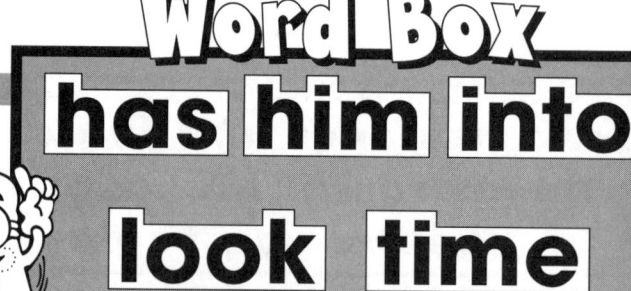

Word Box
has him into
look time

Can you read and spell these words?

Read, whisper and finger-clap the words in the word box before you begin.

1. Trace the grey words and frames around each word from the word box. Draw a frame around each matching word.

look	look	like	late
him	him	how	had
into	is	into	it
has	had	have	has
time	that	there	time

2. Find the words from the word box. Frame the word. Write the word in the open frame and trace the frame.

into	if	it	
had	has	have	
then	this	time	
look	like	live	
he	him	hit	

Teacher's Friend Publications, Inc. ©   50   TF2425 Word Wall Practice! High Frequency Words Level 1

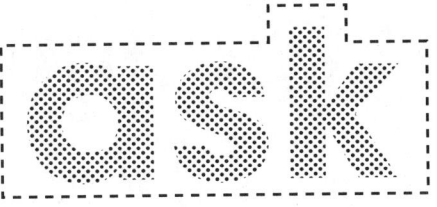 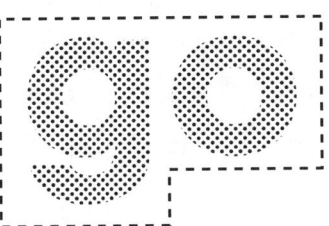

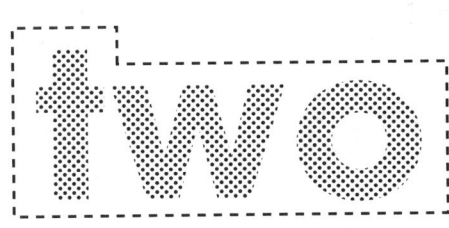 

High Frequency Word Cards

For each word:
- ☐ Trace the word.
- ☐ Trace the frame.

Cut the word cards apart and practice reading the words with a friend.

Name _____

Word Box
ask go more see two

Read, whisper and finger-clap the words in the word box before you begin.

Write the words from the word box and draw a frame around each word.

1. _____
2. _____
3. _____
4. _____
5. _____

Can you read and spell these words?

6. Unscramble this word from the word box.

o r m e

_____

7. Circle the words from the word box and place an "X" on each word that does *not* appear in the word box.

go	gone
and	ask
she	see
make	more
two	that

Now, turn this page over and write the words from the word box from memory. Did you spell each word correctly?

Teacher's Friend Publications, Inc. ©   52   TF2425 Word Wall Practice! High Frequency Words Level 1

Name _____

Word Box
ask go more
see two

Read, whisper and finger-clap the words in the word box before you begin.

Read each sentence.
Find a word from the word box in each sentence and circle it.

Can you read and spell these words?

1. Please ask before you leave.

2. You need two pins.

3. We can get one more.

4. I can see you there.

5. We all may go now.

6. Unscramble these words from the word box.

o w t _____

e s e _____

s k a _____

Teacher's Friend Publications, Inc. ©   53   TF2425 Word Wall Practice! High Frequency Words Level 1

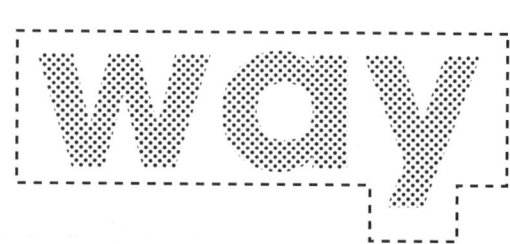

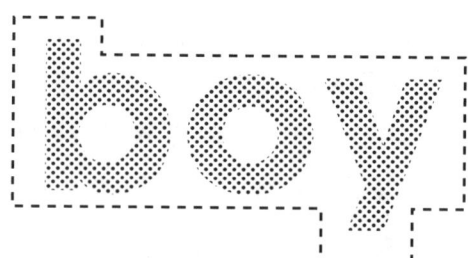

High Frequency Word Cards

For each word:
- ☐ Trace the word.
- ☐ Trace the frame.

Cut the word cards apart and practice reading the words with a friend.

Teacher's Friend Publications, Inc. ©   54   TF2425 Word Wall Practice! High Frequency Words Level 1

Name _____

Word Box
big boy no could way

Read, whisper and finger-clap the words in the word box before you begin.

Write the words from the word box and draw a frame around each word.

1. _____
2. _____
3. _____
4. _____
5. _____

Can you read and spell these words?

6. Unscramble this word from the word box.

o u c d l

_____

SPELL ✓
Now, turn this page over and write the words from the word box from memory. Did you spell each word correctly?

7. Find 5 words from the word box in the puzzle. Circle the words.

n	b	p	t	x	b	w	a	y
o	i	c	c	o	u	l	d	w
a	g	g	c	a	l	b	s	k
a	b	o	y	j	u	e	x	h

Teacher's Friend Publications, Inc. ©   55   TF2425 Word Wall Practice! High Frequency Words Level 1

Name _____

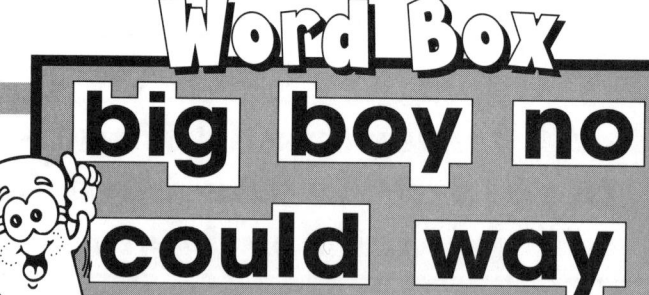

Read, whisper and finger-clap the words in the word box before you begin.

Trace the gray letters and add the missing letters to make each word from the word box. Trace the frame around each word.

Can you read and spell these words?

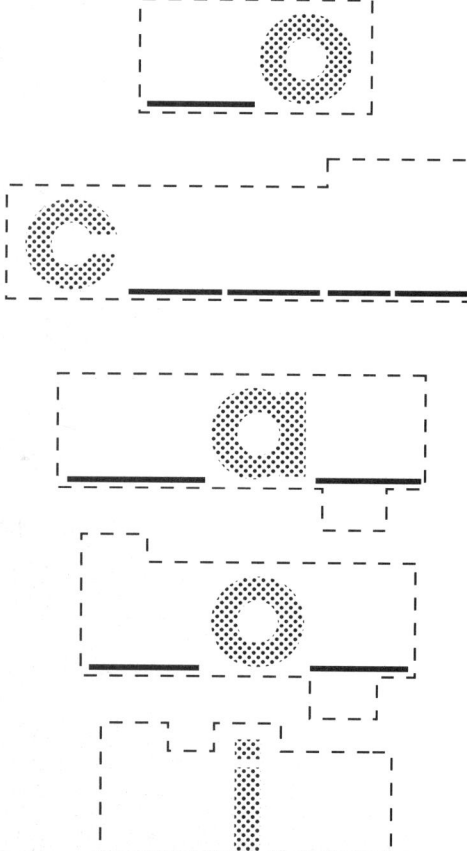

1.
2.
3.
4.
5.

Bonus Activity!

Circle the word in the sentence below that also appears in the word box.

It could work out well.

6. Circle the words below that appear in the word box. Place an "X" on each word that does not appear in the word box. (Words may appear more than once.)

way	more	no	could
two	could	boy	big
boy	make	big	way
no	boy	could	many

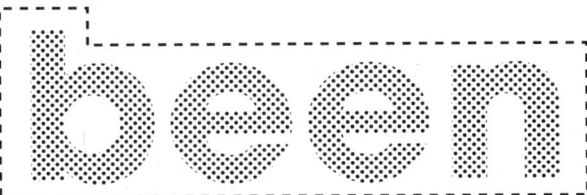
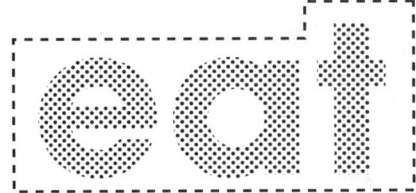
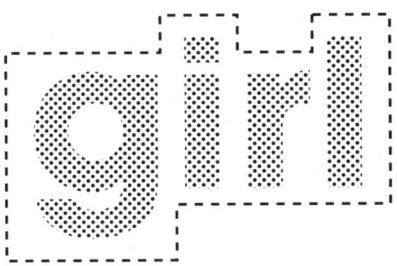
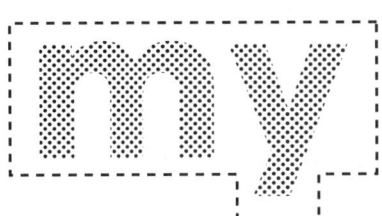
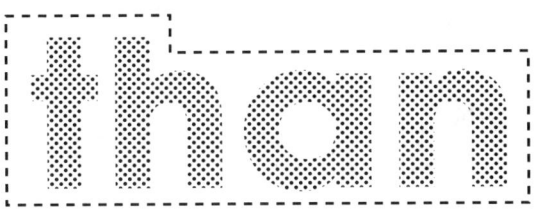

High Frequency Word Cards

For each word:
- ☐ Trace the word.
- ☐ Trace the frame.

Cut the word cards apart and practice reading the words with a friend.

Name _____

Read, whisper and finger-clap the words in the word box before you begin.

Word Box
been eat girl my than

Write the words from the word box and draw a frame around each word.

1. _____
2. _____
3. _____
4. _____
5. _____

6. Unscramble this word from the word box.

r l i g

Can you read and spell these words?

7. Circle the words from the word box and place an "X" on each word that does *not* appear in the word box.

eat   each

my   many

the   than

girl   go

big   been

SPELL

Now, turn this page over and write the words from the word box from memory. Did you spell each word correctly?

Teacher's Friend Publications, Inc. ©   58   TF2425 Word Wall Practice! High Frequency Words Level 1

Name _____

Word Box
been eat girl
my than

Read, whisper and finger-clap the words in the word box before you begin.

Can you read and spell these words?

1. Trace the grey words and frames around each word from the word box. Draw a frame around each matching word.

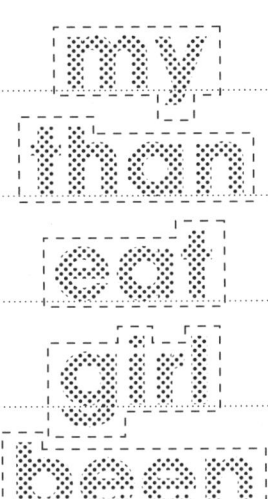

my	many	make
there	than	they
eat	ask	each
go	one	girl
by	been	be

2. Find the words from the word box. Frame the word. Write the word in the open frame and trace the frame.

girl	like	she
eat	are	ask
the	they	than
but	been	how
not	my	you

Teacher's Friend Publications, Inc. ©   59   TF2425 Word Wall Practice! High Frequency Words Level 1

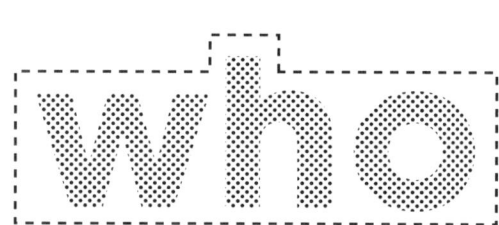 

High Frequency Word Cards

For each word:
- ☐ Trace the word.
- ☐ Trace the frame.

Cut the word cards apart and practice reading the words with a friend.

Name _____

Word Box
**call car find
now who**

Read, whisper and finger-clap the words in the word box before you begin.

Write the words from the word box and draw a frame around each word.

1. _____
2. _____
3. _____
4. _____
5. _____

Can you read and spell these words?

6. Unscramble this word from the word box.

d f n i

_____

SPELL ✓

Now, turn this page over and write the words from the word box from memory. Did you spell each word correctly?

7. Find 5 words from the word box in the puzzle. Circle the words.

f d n t c f i n d
w h o c a a b j c
a e w r l b b s a
a b b c l t e x r

Teacher's Friend Publications, Inc. ©   61   TF2425 Word Wall Practice! High Frequency Words Level 1

Name _____

Word Box
call car find now who

Read, whisper and finger-clap the words in the word box before you begin.

Read each sentence. Find a word from the word box in each sentence and circle it.

Can you read and spell these words?

1. I will call you later today.
2. We will go home now.
3. I can find the ball.
4. Do you know who he is?
5. I like your new car.

6. Unscramble these words from the word box.

w n o _____

h o w _____

l a c l _____

Teacher's Friend Publications, Inc. ©   TF2425 Word Wall Practice! High Frequency Words Level 1

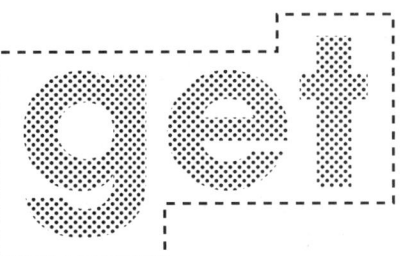

High Frequency Word Cards

For each word:
- ☐ Trace the word.
- ☐ Trace the frame.

Cut the word cards apart and practice reading the words with a friend.

Teacher's Friend Publications, Inc. ©   63   TF2425 Word Wall Practice! High Frequency Words Level 1

Name _____

Word Box
day did down get long

Read, whisper and finger-clap the words in the word box before you begin.

Write the words from the word box and draw a frame around each word.

1. _____
2. _____
3. _____
4. _____
5. _____

Can you read and spell these words?

7. Circle the words from the word box and place an "X" on each word that does *not* appear in the word box.

get   girl
big   down
look long
day   do
did   but

6. Unscramble this word from the word box.

o n w d

_____

Now, turn this page over and write the words from the word box from memory. Did you spell each word correctly?

Name _____

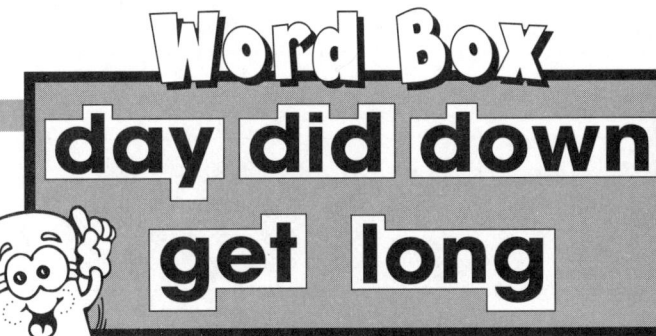

Word Box
day did down
get long

Read, whisper and finger-clap the words in the word box before you begin.

Trace the gray letters and add the missing letters to make each word from the word box. Trace the frame around each word.

Can you read and spell these words?

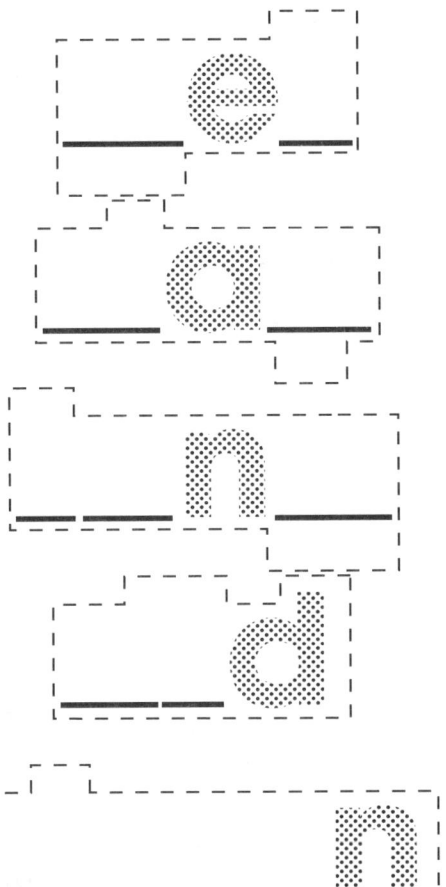

1. _ e _
2. _ a _
3. _ n _
4. _ _ d
5. _ _ _ n

Bonus Activity!

Circle the word in the sentence below that also appears in the word box.

He did a good job.

6. Circle the words below that appear in the word box. Place an "X" on each word that does not appear in the word box. (Words may appear more than once.)

long	look	get	down
do	did	day	but
get	down	each	long
day	girl	did	like

Teacher's Friend Publications, Inc. ©

come

good

made

may

part

High Frequency Word Cards

For each word:
- ☐ Trace the word.
- ☐ Trace the frame.

Cut the word cards apart and practice reading the words with a friend.

Name

Word Box
come good made may part

Read, whisper and finger-clap the words in the word box before you begin.

Write the words from the word box and draw a frame around each word.

1. _____
2. _____
3. _____
4. _____
5. _____

Can you read and spell these words?

6. Unscramble this word from the word box.

o e m c

_____

SPELL ✓
Now, turn this page over and write the words from the word box from memory. Did you spell each word correctly?

7. Find 5 words from the word box in the puzzle. Circle the words.

f	m	a	d	e	b	p	g	p
v	a	c	c	c	o	m	e	a
a	y	g	o	o	d	r	s	r
a	b	b	c	j	u	t	x	t

Teacher's Friend Publications, Inc. © 67 TF2425 Word Wall Practice! High Frequency Words Level 1

Name _____

Read, whisper and finger-clap the words in the word box before you begin.

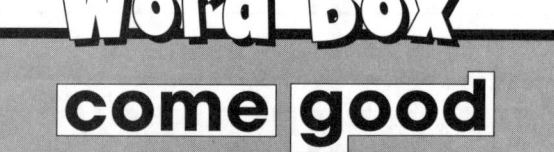

Word Box
come good
made may part

Can you read and spell these words?

1. Trace the grey words and frames around each word from the word box. Draw a frame around each matching word.

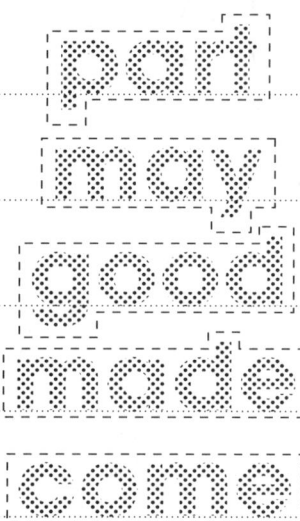

about	part	girl
make	my	may
down	good	go
made	many	mile
come	call	can

2. Find the words from the word box. Frame the word. Write the word in the open frame and trace the frame.

good	been	go
pull	about	part
not	made	day
could	come	can
make	my	may

Teacher's Friend Publications, Inc. ©   TF2425 Word Wall Practice! High Frequency Words Level 1

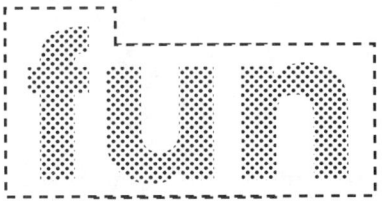

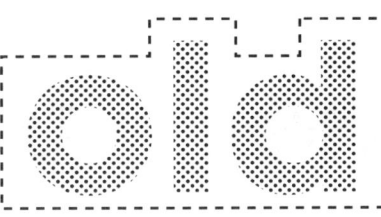

High Frequency Word Cards

For each word:
- ☐ Trace the word.
- ☐ Trace the frame.

Cut the word cards apart and practice reading the words with a friend.

Name _____

Word Box
fun   here   new
off   old

Read, whisper and finger-clap the words in the word box before you begin.

Write the words from the word box and draw a frame around each word.

1. _____
2. _____
3. _____
4. _____
5. _____

Can you read and spell these words?

7. Circle the words from the word box and place an "X" on each word that does *not* appear in the word box.

new   how
one   off
on   old
fun   for
her   here

6. Unscramble this word from the word box.

r e e h

_____

SPELL

Now, turn this page over and write the words from the word box from memory. Did you spell each word correctly?

Name _____

Read, whisper and finger-clap the words in the word box before you begin.

Word Box
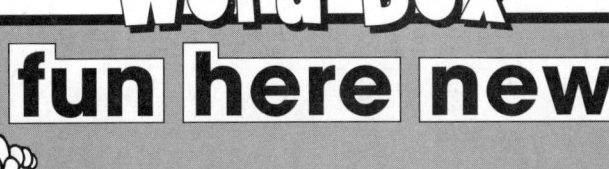
fun here new
off old

Read each sentence.
Find a word from the word box in each sentence and circle it.

Can you read and spell these words?

1. I have a new book about cars.

2. You can put the cake here.

3. We had fun at school today.

4. Please turn the light off.

5. How old are you?

6. Unscramble these words from the word box.

w n e _____

d o l _____

u f n _____

Teacher's Friend Publications, Inc. ©   71   TF2425 Word Wall Practice! High Frequency Words Level 1

run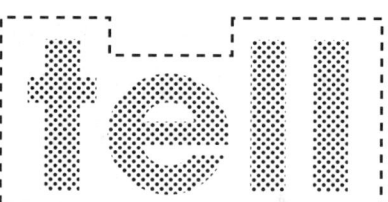

us

why

High Frequency Word Cards

For each word:
  ☐ Trace the word.
  ☐ Trace the frame.

Cut the word cards apart and practice reading the words with a friend.

Name _____

Word Box
run tell us
went why

Read, whisper and finger-clap the words in the word box before you begin.

Write the words from the word box and draw a frame around each word.

1. _____
2. _____
3. _____
4. _____
5. _____

Can you read and spell these words?

6. Unscramble this word from the word box.

n w t e

_____

SPELL ✓

Now, turn this page over and write the words from the word box from memory. Did you spell each word correctly?

7. Find 5 words from the word box in the puzzle. Circle the words.

f d p w x b h u s
v q c e r a b j w
a e g n a b b s h
r u n t e l x y

Teacher's Friend Publications, Inc. ©   73   TF2425 Word Wall Practice! High Frequency Words Level 1

Name _____

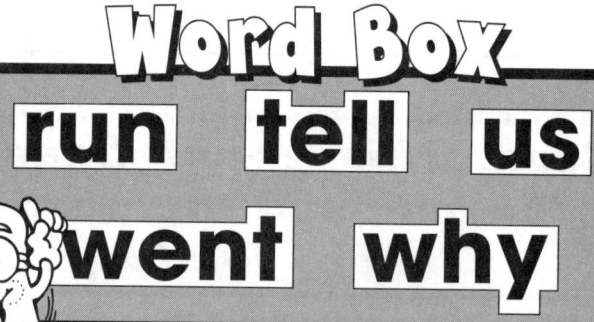

Word Box
run　tell　us
went　why

Read, whisper and finger-clap the words in the word box before you begin.

Trace the gray letters and add the missing letters to make each word from the word box. Trace the frame around each word.

Can you read and spell these words?

1. _ n _
2. _ e _
3. ▢
4. w _ _
5. _ _ n _

Bonus Activity!

Circle the word in the sentence below that also appears in the word box.

She can run fast.

6. Circle the words below that appear in the word box. Place an "X" on each word that does not appear in the word box. (Words may appear more than once.)

us	was	went	tell
as	run	why	this
tell	who	us	run
went	were	what	why

Teacher's Friend Publications, Inc. ©　　74　　TF2425 Word Wall Practice! High Frequency Words Level 1

High Frequency Word Cards

For each word:
- ☐ Trace the word.
- ☐ Trace the frame.

Cut the word cards apart and practice reading the words with a friend.

Name _____

Word Box

give me over
saw want

Read, whisper and finger-clap the words in the word box before you begin.

Write the words from the word box and draw a frame around each word.

1. _____
2. _____
3. _____
4. _____
5. _____

Can you read and spell these words?

7. Circle the words from the word box and place an "X" on each word that does *not* appear in the word box.

saw   some
give get
were want
over out
my   me

6. Unscramble this word from the word box.

v r o e

_____

SPELL ✓

Now, turn this page over and write the words from the word box from memory. Did you spell each word correctly?

Teacher's Friend Publications, Inc. ©   76   TF2425 Word Wall Practice! High Frequency Words Level 1

Name _____

Read, whisper and finger-clap the words in the word box before you begin.

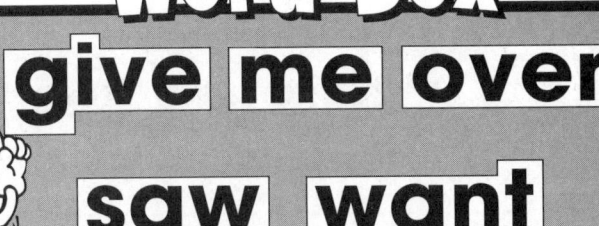

Word Box
give me over
saw want

Can you read and spell these words?

1. Trace the grey words and frames around each word from the word box. Draw a frame around each matching word.

saw	saw	said	she
over	one	old	over
give	get	give	girl
me	more	we	me
want	with	want	when

2. Find the words from the word box. Frame the word. Write the word in the open frame and trace the frame.

me	may	not	
want	will	what	
see	was	saw	
go	give	good	
old	over	of	

Teacher's Friend Publications, Inc. © 77 TF2425 Word Wall Practice! High Frequency Words Level 1

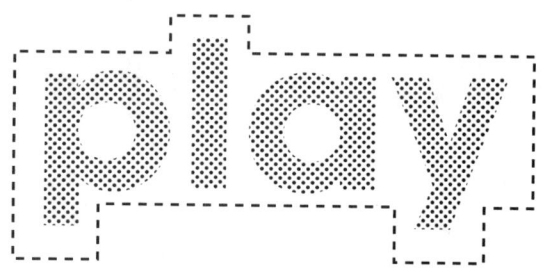 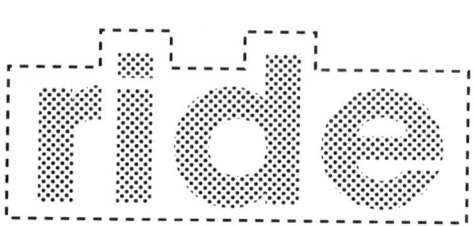

High Frequency Word Cards

For each word:
- ☐ Trace the word.
- ☐ Trace the frame.

Cut the word cards apart and practice reading the words with a friend.

Name _____

Word Box
after am play
ride where

Read, whisper and finger-clap the words in the word box before you begin.

Write the words from the word box and draw a frame around each word.

1. _____
2. _____
3. _____
4. _____
5. _____

Can you read and spell these words?

6. Unscramble this word from the word box.

a p y l

_____

SPELL

Now, turn this page over and write the words from the word box from memory. Did you spell each word correctly?

7. Find 5 words from the word box in the puzzle. Circle the words.

a	f	t	e	r	b	h	g	r
v	q	c	c	a	m	b	j	i
p	l	a	y	s	b	b	s	d
a	b	b	c	w	h	e	r	e

Teacher's Friend Publications, Inc. ©   TF2425 Word Wall Practice! High Frequency Words Level 1

Name _____

Word Box
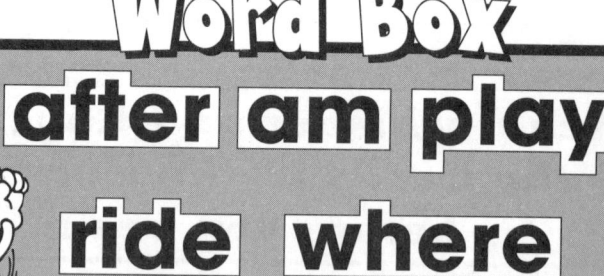
after am play
ride where

Read, whisper and finger-clap the words in the word box before you begin.

Read each sentence.
Find a word from the word box in each sentence and circle it.

Can you read and spell these words?

1. I like to ride my bike.

2. Where is my red ball?

3. I am going home.

4. We can go after school.

5. Do you like to play tag?

6. Unscramble these words from the word box.

e r i d _____

r f t e a _____

e e r h w _____

Teacher's Friend Publications, Inc. ©   80   TF2425 Word Wall Practice! High Frequency Words Level 1

 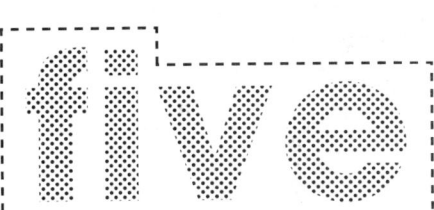

High Frequency Word Cards

For each word:
- ☐ Trace the word.
- ☐ Trace the frame.

Cut the word cards apart and practice reading the words with a friend.

Name _____

Word Box
zero one two
three four five

Read, whisper and finger-clap the words in the word box before you begin.

Write the words from the word box and draw a frame around each word.

1. _____
2. _____
3. _____
4. _____
5. _____
6. _____

Can you read and spell these words?

7. Write the word that matches the numeral.

2 _____
4 _____
0 _____
3 _____
1 _____
5 _____

8. Unscramble this word from the word box.

e r h e t

_____

SPELL

Now, turn this page over and write the words from the word box from memory. Did you spell each word correctly?

Teacher's Friend Publications, Inc. ©   82   TF2425 Word Wall Practice! High Frequency Words Level 1

Name _____

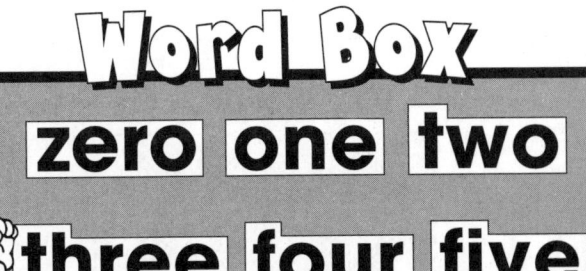

Word Box
zero one two
three four five

Read, whisper and finger-clap the words in the word box before you begin.

Trace the gray letters and add the missing letters to make each word from the word box. Trace the frame around each word.

Can you read and spell these words?

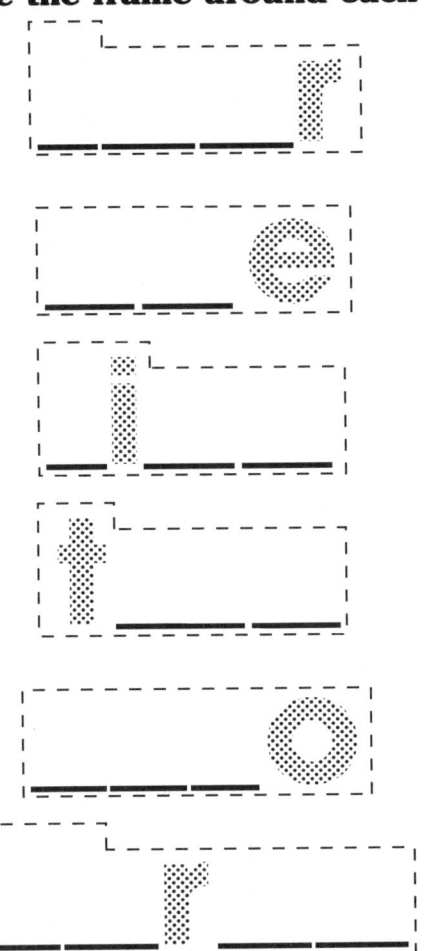

1.
2.
3.
4.
5.

Bonus Activity!

Circle the word in the sentence below that also appears in the word box.

We have three cats.

6. Circle the words below that appear in the word box. Place an "X" on each word that does not appear in the word box. (Words may appear more than once.)

four	five	for	three
to	two	from	four
five	of	zero	on
three	one	old	two

Teacher's Friend Publications, Inc. ©   83   TF2425 Word Wall Practice! High Frequency Words Level 1

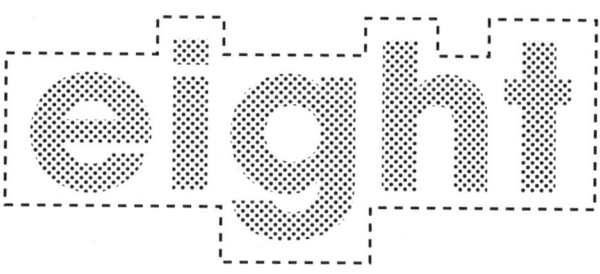
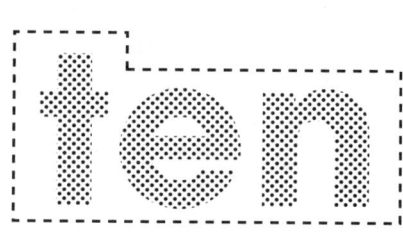

High Frequency Word Cards

For each word:
- ☐ Trace the word.
- ☐ Trace the frame.

Cut the word cards apart and practice reading the words with a friend.

Name _____

Word Box
six   seven   eight
nine   ten

Read, whisper and finger-clap the words in the word box before you begin.

Write the words from the word box and draw a frame around each word.

1. _____
2. _____
3. _____
4. _____
5. _____

Can you read and spell these words?

6. Unscramble this word from the word box.

t i e h g

_____

SPELL

Now, turn this page over and write the words from the word box from memory. Did you spell each word correctly?

7. Find 5 words from the word box in the puzzle. Circle the words.

```
s e v e n b n g t
i q c c r a i j e
x e g r s b n s n
a e i g h t e x h
```

Teacher's Friend Publications, Inc. ©   85   TF2425 Word Wall Practice! High Frequency Words Level 1

Name _____

Read, whisper and finger-clap the words in the word box before you begin.

Word Box
six seven eight
nine ten

Can you read and spell these words?

1. Trace the grey words and frames around each word from the word box. Draw a frame around each matching word.

now	not	nine
see	seven	she
ten	two	to
saw	six	said
eight	eat	each

2. Write the word that matches the numeral.

8 ----------------
10 ----------------
7 ----------------
9 ----------------
6 ----------------

Teacher's Friend Publications, Inc. ©   86   TF2425 Word Wall Practice! High Frequency Words Level 1

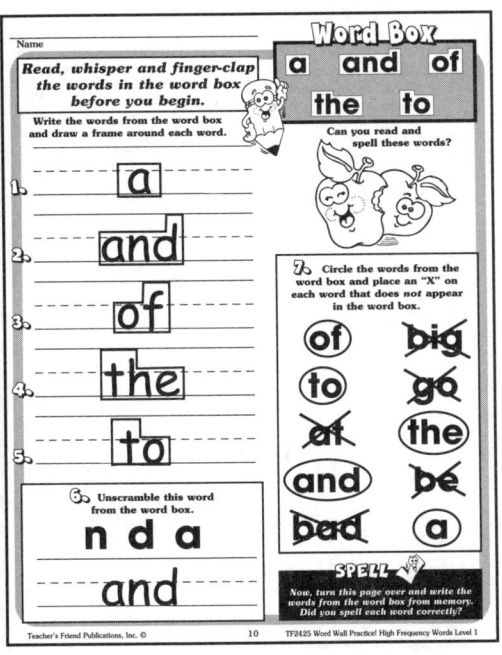

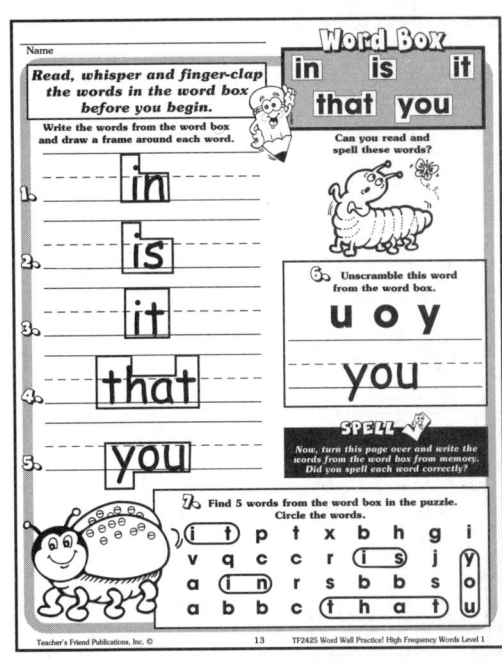
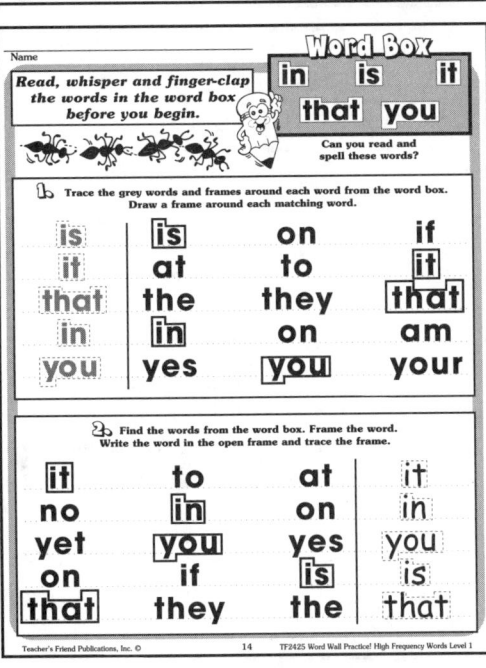

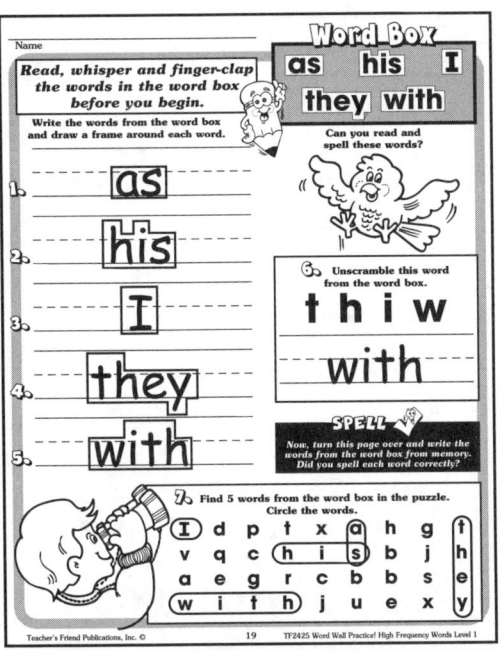
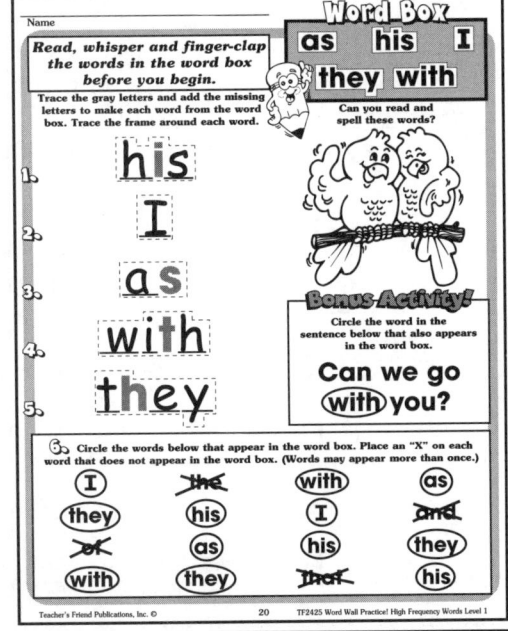
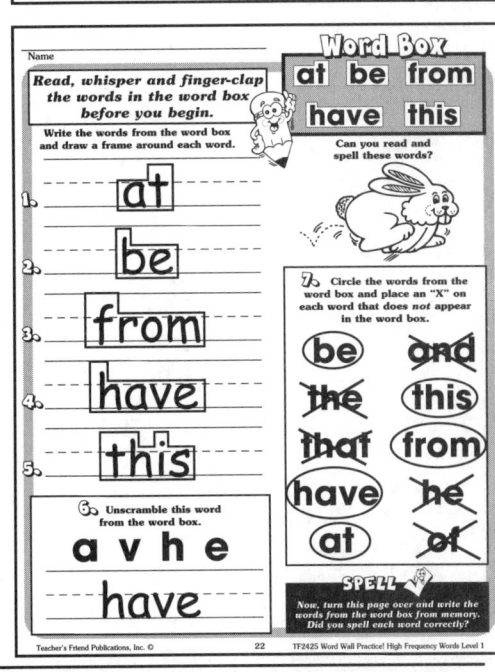

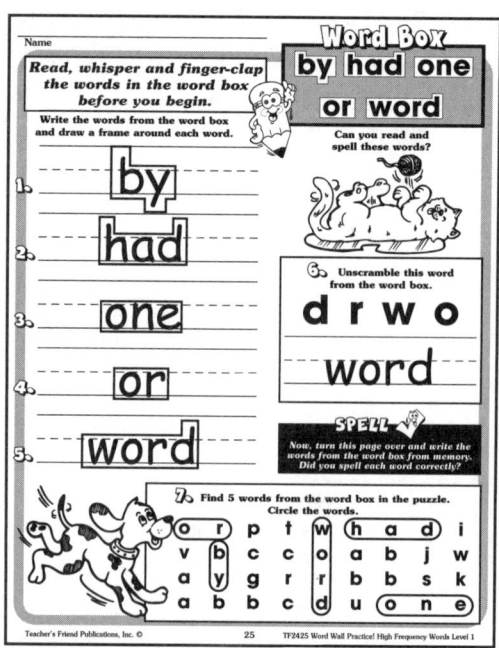
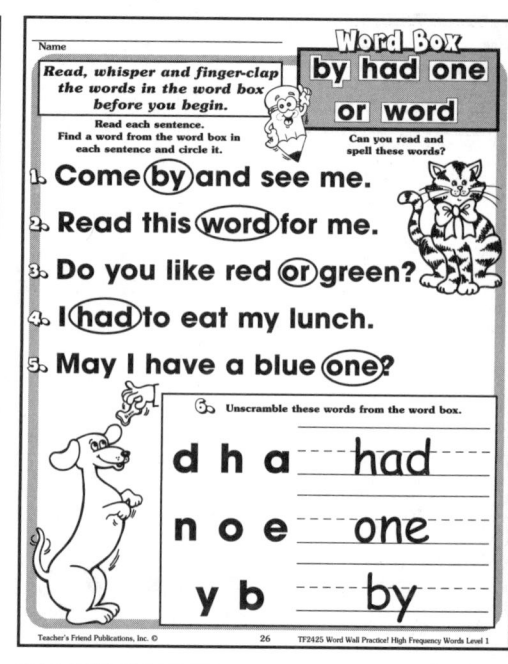

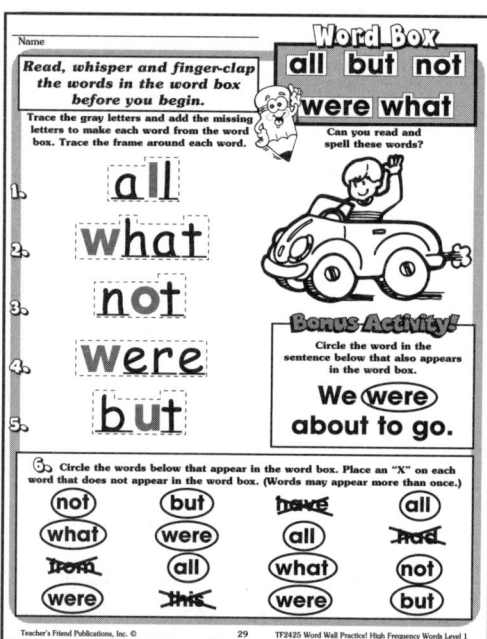
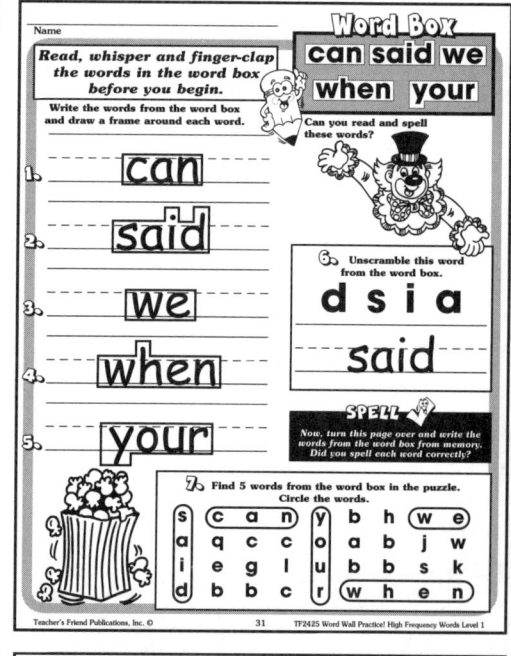

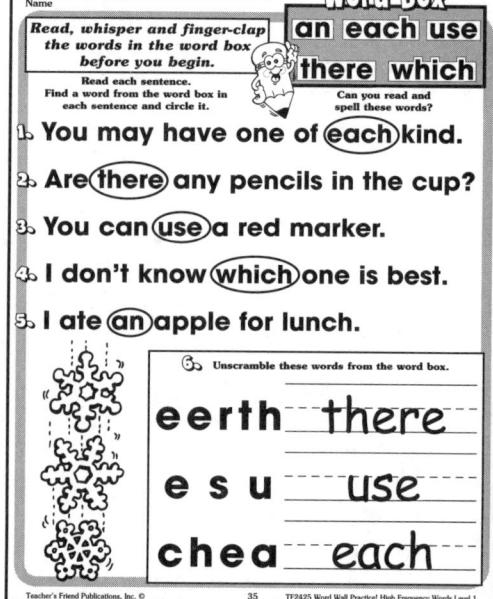

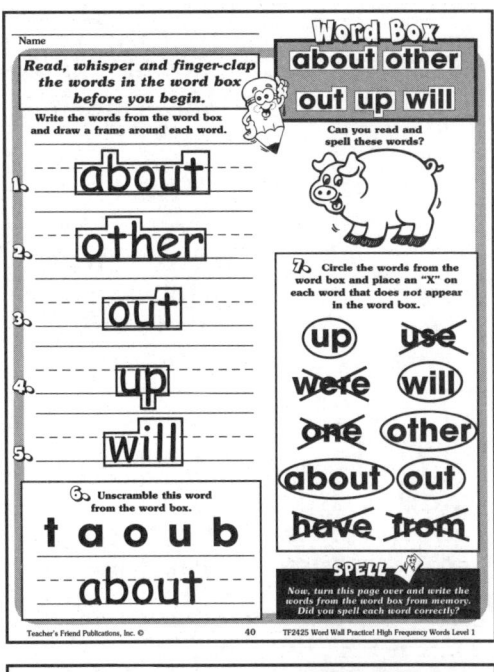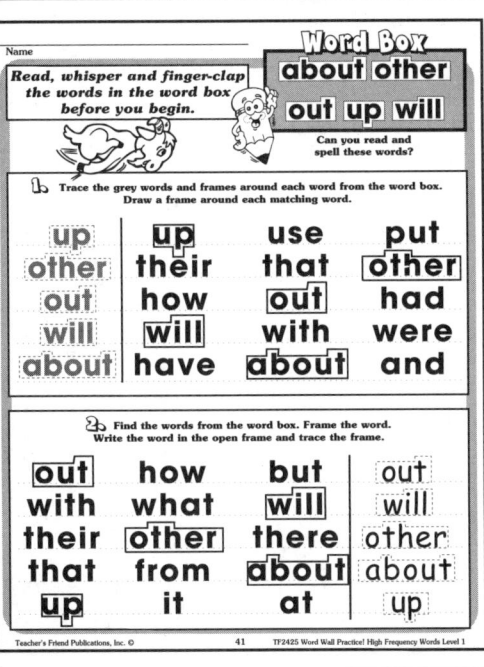

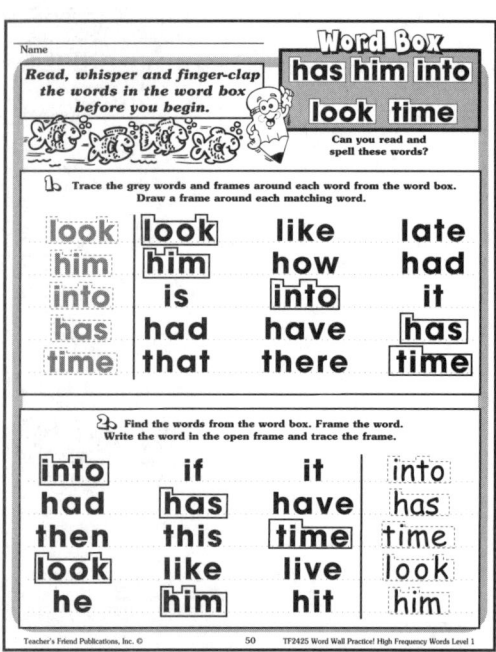
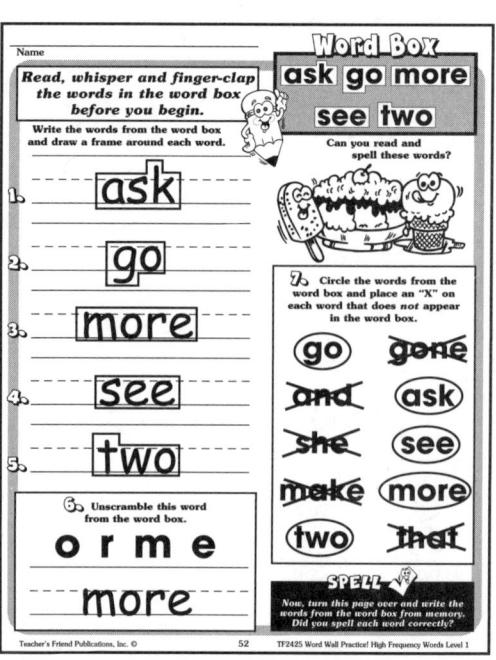

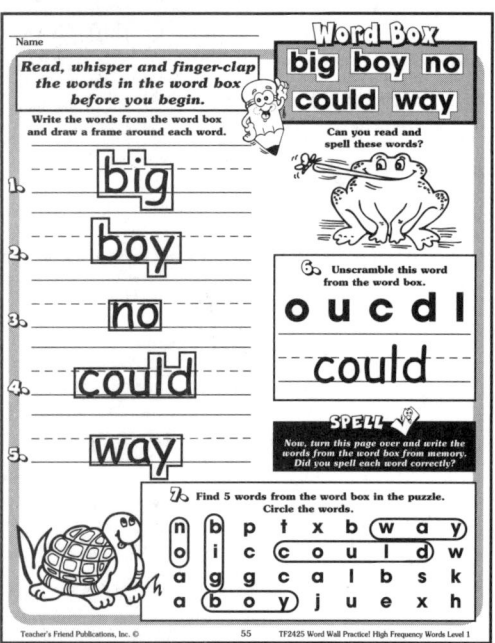
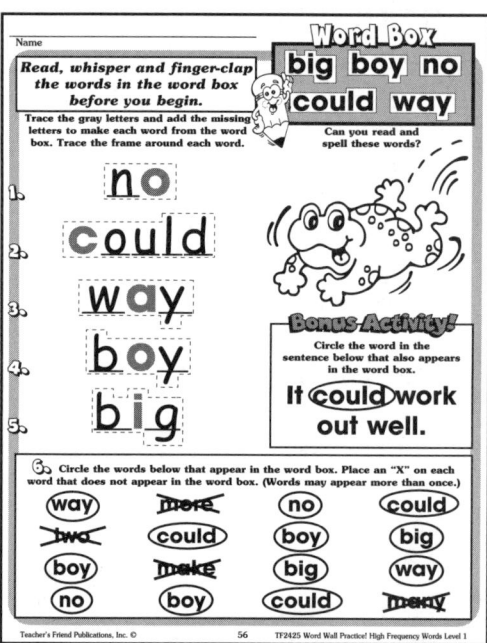

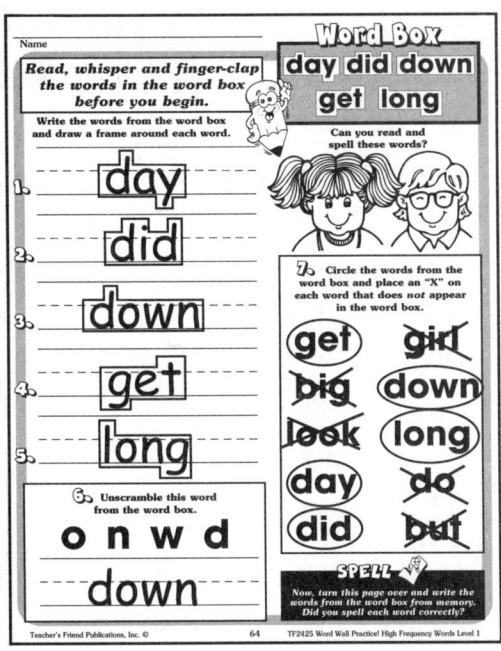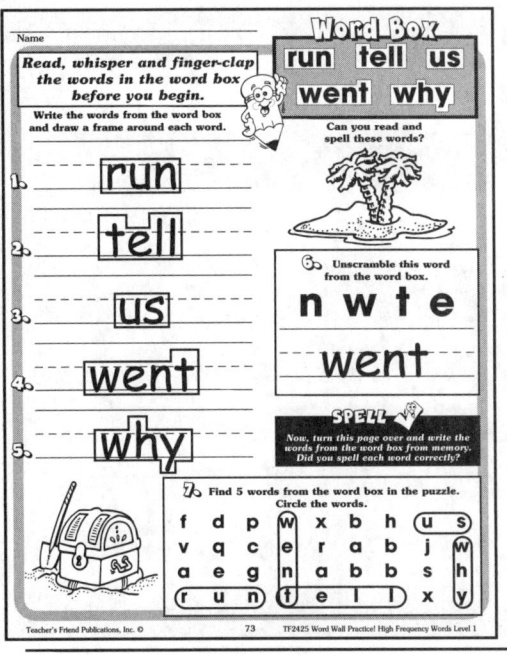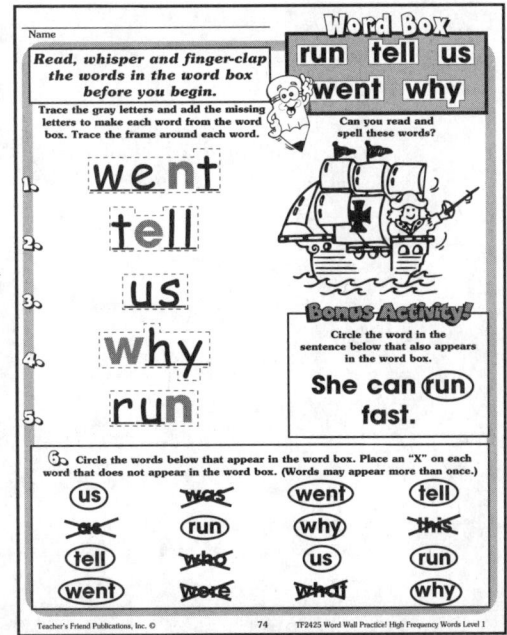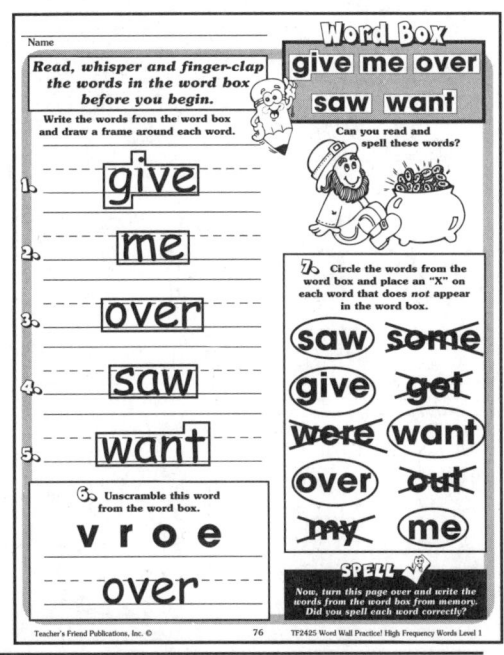

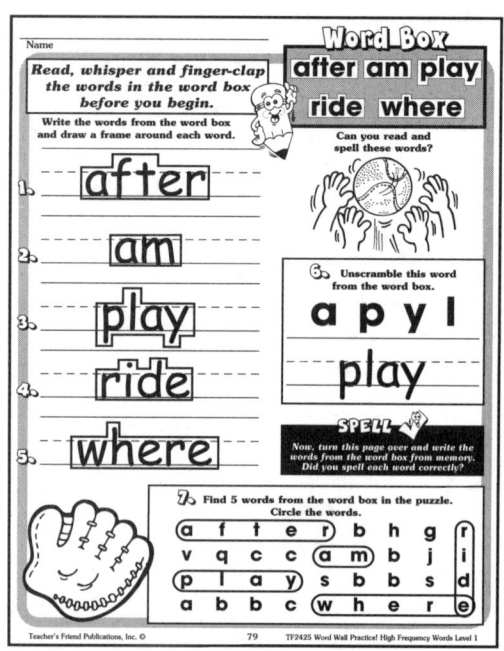
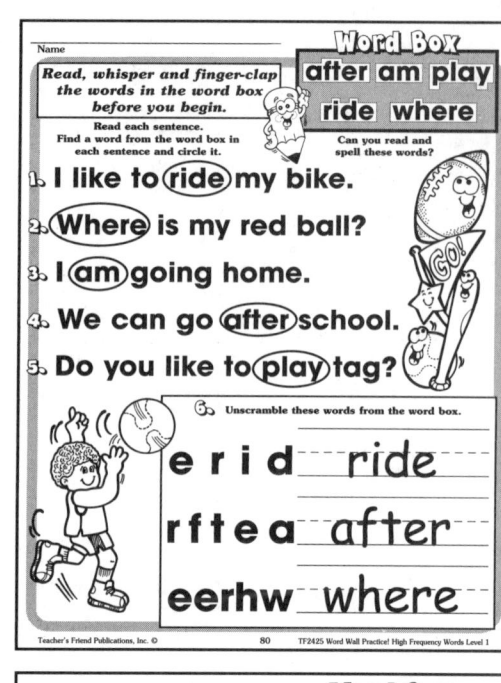

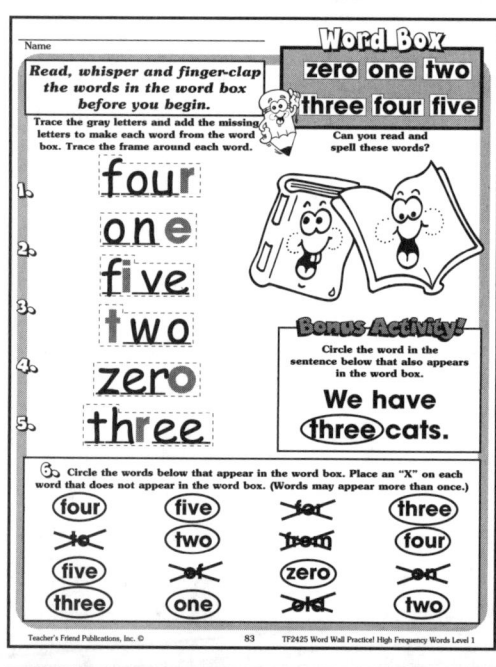

Create-Your-Own Worksheets!

On the next four pages you will find open-ended worksheets to create your own practice sheets for additional or unique words found in your classroom reading materials.

Teacher's Friend Publications, Inc. ©   92   TF2425 Word Wall Practice! High Frequency Words Level 1

Word Box

Name

Read, whisper and finger-clap the words in the word box before you begin.

Write the words from the word box and draw a frame around each word.

1.
2.
3.
4.
5.

6. Unscramble this word from the word box.

Can you read and spell these words?

7. Circle the words from the word box and place an "X" on each word that does *not* appear in the word box.

SPELL ✓

Now, turn this page over and write the words from the word box from memory. Did you spell each word correctly?

Teacher's Friend Publications, Inc. ©   93   TF2425 Word Wall Practice! High Frequency Words Level 1

Name _____

Word Box

Read, whisper and finger-clap the words in the word box before you begin.

Write the words from the word box and draw a frame around each word.

1. _____
2. _____
3. _____
4. _____
5. _____

Can you read and spell these words?

6. Unscramble this word from the word box.

_____
_____

SPELL ✓

Now, turn this page over and write the words from the word box from memory. Did you spell each word correctly?

7. Find the words from the word box in the puzzle. Circle the words.

Teacher's Friend Publications, Inc. ©   94   TF2425 Word Wall Practice! High Frequency Words Level 1

Name _____

Word Box

Read, whisper and finger-clap the words in the word box before you begin.

Trace the gray letters and add the missing letters to make each word from the word box. Trace the frame around each word.

Can you read and spell these words?

1. _____

2. _____

3. _____

4. _____

5. _____

Bonus Activity!

Ask a friend to read the words in the word box while you write them on the back of this sheet.

6. Circle the words below that appear in the word box. Place an "X" on each word that does not appear in the word box. (Words may appear more than once.)

_____
_____
_____
_____

Name _____

Word Box

Read, whisper and finger-clap the words in the word box before you begin.

Read each sentence.
Find a word from the word box in each sentence and circle it.

Can you read and spell these words?

1. _____

2. _____

3. _____

4. _____

5. _____

6. **Unscramble these words from the word box.**